REMARKABLE LGBTQ LIVES™

Harvey MILK

PIONEERING GAY POLITICIAN

CORINNE GRINAPOL

ROSEN PUBLISHING®

New York

REMARKABLE LGBTQ LIVES™

Harvey MILK

PIONEERING GAY POLITICIAN

Published in 2015 by The Rosen Publishing Group, Inc.
29 East 21st Street, New York, NY 10010

Copyright © 2015 by The Rosen Publishing Group, Inc.

First Edition

Library of Congress Cataloging-in-Publication Data

Grinapol, Corinne.
Harvey Milk: pioneering gay politician/Corinne Grinapol.—
First edition.
     pages cm.—(Remarkable LGBTQ lives)
Includes bibliographical references and index.
ISBN 978-1-4777-7899-9 (library bound)
1. Milk, Harvey—Juvenile literature. 2. Politicians—
California—San Francisco—Biography—Juvenile literature.
3. Gay politicians—California—San Francisco—Biography—
Juvenile literature. 4. San Francisco (Calif—Politics and
government—20th century—Juvenile literature. 5. San
Francisco (Calif.)—Biography—Juvenile literature. 6. Gay
liberation movement—California—San Francisco—History—
20th century—Juvenile literature. I. Title.
F869.S353M5454 2014
979.4'61053092—dc23
[B]
                                                    2014010437

Manufactured in China

CONTENTS

INTRO

Harvey Milk lived during a time when being openly gay was dangerous. When a gay person's homosexuality was discovered, he could lose his job, go to jail, or, in some cases, be killed. Although Harvey Milk never hid the fact that he was gay, he preferred to keep his sexuality under wraps in his early years. During his youth and early adulthood, in many ways, Milk was very different from the man he would become later on.

Decades of moving around the country, switching jobs and careers, and years of general restlessness would end when Milk moved to San Francisco for good. There, he finally figured out who he was and what he wanted to do. Milk went from being a man who kept quiet about his homosexuality to a man who fought on behalf of what would come to be known as the gay and lesbian community. He went from being a man who supported Republican politicians to someone who became a politician himself—a liberal one.

Once Harvey Milk got his first chance to run for office, he knew that this was what he was meant to do. Despite some early defeats, Milk never gave up,

DUCTION

Harvey Milk's political career and ambitions were cut short when he was tragically assassinated in 1978, but his story continues to inspire new generations.

and his persistence would lead him to become San Francisco's first openly gay elected politician.

Sadly, Milk's life was cut short when he was assassinated less than a year after his election, but despite his short time in office, he would make an impact that is still felt today.

Harvey Milk became a symbol of inspiration and hope for the gay and lesbian community, both during his life and after. He spent so little time in office, so many years of his life unsure of himself, unsure of what he was meant to do, yet he radically transformed both himself and his community.

THE EARLY YEARS

Harvey Bernard Milk was born on May 22, 1930, at Woodmere General Hospital, Long Island, New York. He was the younger of two sons born to Minerva and William Milk. The Milk last name hadn't existed in Harvey Milk's family until his grandfather, Morris Milch, immigrated from Lithuania to the United States, at which point the name was changed from Milch to Milk.

Harvey Milk grew up in Woodmere, a suburban community on Long Island. He was an unusual kid. There was his appearance, for example. He had big features: big ears, big feet, and a big nose. He would get teased for his looks, but Harvey knew how to fight back with humor and liked the attention he got from making people laugh. He loved opera. When he was young, Harvey would tune into radio broadcasts of opera performances. When he was in junior high school, he switched from listening on the radio

A row of houses line
a residential block in
Woodmere, Long Island.

to listening live. He would take the Long Island Railroad into Manhattan, where he took in performances at the Metropolitan Opera House in the standing-room-only section. It was around this time that Harvey started to realize he might be gay.

The Milk family moved to Bay Shore, Long Island, for Harvey's high school years. Bay Shore is an hour farther from Manhattan but opened Harvey up to an entirely new world. Bay Shore had ferry service to Fire Island, a popular vacation spot for actors, writers, and the wealthy. Harvey would sometime take trips to the island to explore a world of people unlike the ones he knew from his middle-class suburban world.

At Bay Shore High School, Harvey remained firmly in the closet to avoid potential bullying. He was involved in multiple sports, such as being a linebacker for the junior varsity football team and playing basketball, for which his height was an advantage. Harvey wasn't particularly gifted at sports, but he worked hard. He worked hard in academics as well and graduated a year early in June 1947.

AN EDUCATION

Milk attended New York State College for Teachers at Albany, now known as the State University of New York at Albany. He majored in math and

Albany, New York, is home to SUNY Albany, where Milk attended college, and SUNY Plaza, the seat of administration for the entire New York system.

minored in history, planning to become a teacher
when he graduated. His interest in sports followed
him to college, and he quickly involved himself in
campus life. He played on intramural teams in basketball, volleyball, and softball, and wrote about
sports for the college paper, *State College News*. He
also joined Kappa Beta, a Jewish fraternity, and he
was the coach of his fraternity's intramural basketball
team during his junior year. While at college, Milk
suffered his first political defeat: a run for freshman
class president. Although Milk's main focus for the
paper was sports, his interest in politics was growing. He wrote opinion pieces on issues important to
him, such as an article against hazing. It wasn't his
extracurricular activities, however, that made Milk
memorable to his classmates years later—it was his
outgoing nature and outsized personality.

Harvey Milk graduated college in June 1951,
but his path from graduation to teaching was inter-
rupted by world events. By the time Milk graduated,
war had broken out in Korea, and the United States
was involved in helping the South Koreans face off
against the Communists in the North. For Milk, there
was little doubt about enlisting. The war was a chance
to fulfill his patriotic duty and stop the Communists.
He enlisted in the United States Navy, quickly moving
up the ranks until he became the chief petty officer
of submarine rescue vessel USS *Kittiwake*. Serving

stateside throughout the war, he was later stationed in San Diego, where he served as a deep-sea diving instructor, an activity he greatly enjoyed.

Milk was discharged from the navy almost four years after enlisting (he later said that he was dishonorably discharged due to his homosexuality, but military records do not support this claim). He then began the career path for which he had prepared in college. He became a teacher near his original hometown, at George W. Hewlett High School in Hewlett, New York, though his teaching career wouldn't last long. During this time, Milk met the man with whom he would have the longest romantic relationship of his life.

FIRST LOVE

In 1956 at a beach in Queens, New York, Milk, twenty-six at the time and still teaching, met Joe Campbell, a nineteen-year-old whose family had moved to New York five years earlier. A few weeks after meeting, they started dating, and Campbell moved into Milk's apartment in Rego Park, Queens. The fact that they were both men wasn't the only thing unusual about their relationship for that time: Milk was Jewish, and Campbell was Christian. Campbell's family, however, welcomed Milk into their family. Campbell was also accepted by Milk's family, although their homosexuality was never discussed by either family.

Harvey Milk and Joe Campbell relax on the beach. They first met at Jacob Riis Park, a popular beach destination in New York City.

Milk and Campbell felt comfortable with each other very quickly. Milk wrote love poems to Campbell, and each surprised the other with little gifts. They added baby talk to their conversations. When they left notes or wrote letters to each other, they added "san" to the end of their names, which is a sign of respect in Japanese culture.

LOVE LETTERS: SELECTIONS FROM HARVEY MILK'S LETTERS TO JOE CAMPBELL

Although Milk and Campbell's relationship ended, their contact with each other did not. In 1993, Campbell donated letters Milk had written between 1961 and 1964 to the Gay and Lesbian Center of the San Francisco Public Library. Below are some excerpts.

In 1961:
    ...I'm so sorry that we are not together & wish so much to hold you once again—forgive me for writing as I have but I do feel like I do have a truly broken heart—I miss you—I love you—I want you— As Always Love Harveysan

In 1962, writing from Puerto Rico
    Dear Joe—How does one describe the indescribable? Can I take a picture with a wide (extrawide) angle lens using the most sensitive film & then I show it to you to try to explain the feel of the wind as it gently flows over the mountain tops to brush against your face & how does one tell about the odors that vary from moment to moment like the taste of a mango—this is all part of San Juan & the 30 miles around it that I've seen...

In the same letter, describing his sense of the Puerto Ricans:
    ...they have a family unity, & above all a smile—sense of humor & a most pleasant disposition—so unlike those

(continued on the next page)

(continued from the previous page)

in N.Y. who have been thrown together, stepped on & beaten down until they react like a kicked dog—there is a difference that can not be explained—it must be seen—& the color, streets, noise, beauty can never...be explained— only felt. This to me so far is San Juan—this & the million dollar hotels & gambling casinos & the grand restaurants & the most handsome group of people...

In 1963, while looking for work in Miami:
My neurotic self and I have arrived at third rate Viriginian Hotel in most jam packed and slightly gay Miami Beach. Work seems to be available for non jewish and non spanish speaking individuals must confess that I like this warm warm weather and crotons. Regards to all the boys. Harvey

In 1963, writing from Miami about the dangers of being outed:
...Was offered one halfway decent job at $92 per week for a small insurance company but turned it down, for it was not what I would really like—not that I know what I would like, but the people that I would have worked for looked too catty and small townish, and that is bad in Miami—the police here are always after the gay set—raiding the bars (which is unlike NY's raids—here they take in most of the people and publish the names in the newspaper)—they also put out plants as hitchhikers, and in coffee shops, and some-times even raid the gay beach!!!!

Although the two faced few problems with their families, being gay in the 1950s was problematic and potentially dangerous. One of the reasons they had to keep their relationship secret was Milk's job as a high school teacher and after-school basket-ball coach. In those days, being gay—or even being suspected of being gay—was grounds for firing. But even if that wasn't a factor, Milk was losing interest in teaching. He considered quitting but was unsure of what he wanted to do with the rest of his professional career. What he *was* sure about, however, was that he had grown tired of the cold New York winters. In 1957, a twenty-seven-year-old Milk and twenty-year-old Campbell moved to Dallas, Texas, making the trip in a new Plymouth Savoy.

THE WANDER YEARS

In Dallas, Milk discovered that it was hard to find employment, especially for someone who was Jewish. Milk's first job there, as assistant credit manager at a department store, seemed promising but didn't last long. The owner's son needed a job, so Milk was let go. After that, the opportunities only got worse. Milk worked briefly selling sewing machines, but he realized it was a scam; the machines were expensive and the people who bought them couldn't keep up with the monthly payments, so the machines were repossessed and resold. Just half a year after they had moved, Milk and Campbell returned to New York.

They rented an apartment on East 96th Street in Manhattan. Milk got a job as an actuarial assistant at an insurance company, analyzing statistics to

This photo of East 100th Street in Manhattan, taken around the time Milk lived in the area, is just blocks away from Milk's 96th Street apartment building.

determine and prevent worst-case scenario situations. Milk and Campbell settled into city life, but things were far from settled. That brief move to Dallas was the first in a series of moves and career changes Milk would make in the next few years. Another big change came in 1962: Milk asked Campbell to move out of the apartment. Their relationship was over.

Soon after, Milk, tired of his job, made another career change. He once again put his math skills to use as a researcher for an investment firm. He was good at his job but was, as with his other jobs, not crazy about it.

Before long, he made another move with the man who was his boyfriend at the time. Milk had heard about the changes happening in San Francisco and that the city was attracting a growing population of gay people. In 1969, Milk decided to check it out for himself. Falling back into a familiar career path, Milk worked for an investment firm in San Francisco.

Milk would come back to New York in 1971 and work in theater as a producer, but the culture of San Francisco had made an impression, and he would soon return to San Francisco for good.

CHAPTER 2

SAN FRANCISCO CALLS

The present-day image of San Francisco is that of a liberal, open city with a sizeable gay population. It wasn't always like that, and Harvey Milk got to witness the changing face of San Francisco for himself. When World War II broke out in 1939, San Francisco had a reputation as a working-class city full of blue-collar workers. People worked in manufacturing, mining, and construction. Working factories dotted the city. San Francisco's population was comprised largely of middle-class families, many of whom were Catholic. While more conservative than it currently is, San Francisco was by no means a traditional, straightlaced city.

As a port city, more than a century of comings and goings had introduced many different types of people to the city and created an air of tolerance. Significant societal changes happened during and immediately after World War II. San Francisco had

23

On modern-day Castro Street in San Francisco, a woman waves a pride flag after a Supreme Court decision effectively ends the ban on same-sex marriage in California.

been a major military port during many wars, dating back to the Spanish-American War in 1898. It continued to be an important port city during World War II on the Pacific front. Military policy

during this war would be an important factor in the changing face of San Francisco. Back then, gays were not allowed in the military. During World War II, this policy was enforced. If a serviceman were

discovered to be gay, he or she would be dishonorably discharged. When this happened, those gay
servicemen often decided to stay in San Francisco
because the city was often a more tolerant place
for them than their hometowns were likely to be.
This is one of the ways San Francisco's gay population began to grow.

The civil and women's rights movements and the
counterculture movements also left their mark on San
Francisco and the country as a whole. Greater open-
ness and acceptance were becoming the norm, and
pockets of San Francisco became incubators for hippie and beatnik culture, which included members of
the gay community.

As cars became more affordable and more and
more highways were built in the 1950s and '60s, the
popularity of suburbs increased. During this time,
factory jobs started to decline. The combination of
those factors led many working-class families to move
out of San Francisco and into the suburbs.

One of the places where such a migration
occurred was San Francisco's Eureka Valley. As families left, homes became empty and housing prices
declined. In 1963, a gay bar opened up in the area,
and then another. Gay San Franciscans, particularly
men, started to move to the Eureka Valley as a result,
converging on an area that would become known as
the Castro, a kind of gay mecca.

SAN FRANCISCO'S GAY ESTABLISHMENT

The late 1950s and early '60s were a hard time for San Francisco's gay community. For one, they were often a target of the police. Gay bars were a popular target of unscrupulous police officers, who would make owners pay the police in exchange for being left alone.

Police could and often would arrest members of the gay and lesbian community for any reason. Police raided bars and arrested customers on charges similar to disorderly conduct, or improper behavior. The charges wouldn't hold up in court, but that wasn't really the point. The point was to shame people. Newspapers would print the names of those arrested, and police would call their families and workplaces. Such actions could be highly damaging, since not everyone arrested was out of the closet. Additionally, there were no workplace protections, so being gay was considered by many to be a legitimate reason for a company to fire an employee.

Because of acts such as these, many in San Francisco's gay community wanted to avoid causing a stir, preferring to stay under the radar rather than fight for rights. However, as raids intensified, some people started changing their minds and considered organizing clubs. The first gay club in San Francisco, founded in 1952, was a local chapter of a national organization called the Mattachine Society, whose goal was to provide a safe space for the gay and lesbian community. In 1955, Dorothy Louise Taliaferro "Del" Martin and Phyllis Ann Lyon created Daughters of Bilitis (DOB), the first social and political organization for lesbians in the United States. Their original goal was to

(continued on the next page)

(continued from the previous page)

create a safe place to party without disruption by police, but they turned more political as they saw the pressure society was exerting on lesbians.

More clubs were to come: the Society for Individual Rights (SIR) and the Alice B. Toklas Memorial Democratic Club, the latter of which was the most directly involved in politics. These clubs invited politicians and candidates running for city positions to come talk to them. At first, no one would come because they were afraid to be associated with the gay and lesbian community. However, as the gay and lesbian community grew stronger as a voting force, it became advantageous to court the gay vote, and politicians would come to the clubs, trying to demonstrate how their policies would help the gay and lesbian community.

By the time Harvey Milk arrived in San Francisco, the clubs were fairly powerful. However, their goal was to initiate a slow and steady race toward gay rights. At the point when Milk wanted to run for office, these clubs were looking to support gay-friendly, rather than gay, candidates. They were afraid to rock the boat too fast or too soon. Even if these clubs had wanted to support a gay candidate for election, Milk wouldn't have been their choice: he was a newcomer and was therefore considered presumptuous for running for political office. Milk, for his part, liked neither the clubs' philosophy nor their opinion of him. Milk's relationship with the clubs would remain uneasy throughout his time in San Francisco.

CASTRO CAMERA

At the beginning of 1972, Milk was back in New York, working as associate producer of a play, but he had had enough. Milk left the play and moved, once again, to California. His boyfriend at the time, Scott Smith, joined him a short while later, and they spent several months driving through California, living off their unemployment income. After almost a year of this, they returned to San Francisco. Milk was almost out of unemployment funds and unsure of what he was going to do to earn money, but he was happy.

Milk and Smith moved to Castro Street because rents were cheap. They were still without jobs, but a mistake at a drugstore would soon change that. Milk had dropped off a roll of film at a pharmacy to be developed. The pharmacy, however, damaged the film and the photos were ruined. Deciding he could do a better job than the pharmacy, Milk and Smith opened a camera store. Part of what Milk liked about the idea of having his own store was its concordance with his own family history; Milk's grandfather and father had each run a department store established by his grandfather.

While Milk might have had some experience running a business, however indirect, neither he nor his boyfriend knew much about cameras or developing film. They were ready to give it a go, however, so they spent the last of their funds, $1,000, on their new business. Five hundred dollars went to buying equipment and supplies, and the other $500 went toward paying their new five-year lease. On March 3, 1973, Castro Camera was officially open for business.

This photo of the Castro, taken a few months after Milk's death, gives an idea of what the neighborhood looked like during his time there.

Castro Camera, 575 Castro Street, would become the center of Harvey Milk's San Francisco life. He and Smith lived in an apartment right above the store, but more important, once Milk decided to go into politics Castro Camera would no longer be simply a camera store. It would serve as his campaign headquarters.

MILK GETS POLITICAL

In a way, Milk's growing interest in politics mirrored the political development and growing clout of San Francisco's gay community. The 1950s and '60s were a time when political movements—civil rights, antiwar, feminist, counterculture—flowered, and it seemed only natural that the gay rights movement would follow. In fact, those movements influenced the gay rights movement.

One of the events that galvanized the movement in San Francisco was the 1959 race for mayor. During the campaign, one of the candidates said the other was permissive toward gay groups in the city. The other candidate denied this claim. Both considered it a negative idea to treat gay groups as legitimate and to accept them into the San Francisco mainstream. This stance turned off a lot of gay people. When the ballots were counted, nine thousand people had voted for neither candidate. This stance was a significant number and an early sign of the growing political importance of the gay community.

Senators listen to testimony during the Watergate hearings from one of the men who broke into the Democratic National Committee headquarters. The hearings would have a profound effect on Milk.

On a personal level, there were three incidents that prompted Milk to jump into the political ring. The first was a visit from a government representative who came into Castro Camera and told Milk that he had to pay a $100 deposit for sales tax in order to be allowed to run his business. Milk, angry at what he believed was the government meddling in business, got into a shouting match with the man.

The second incident was a request from a teacher to borrow a projector from Castro Camera. The San Francisco school district was low on funds, and it would have taken her a month to get a projector, which she needed right away for lessons. Harvey was angered by the contrast between the city that didn't have enough money for schools but did for corporations.

The final incident related to politics on the national level. During that time,

President Richard Nixon's party and close advisers were accused of illegally spying and breaking into the Democratic National Committee headquarters to obtain Democrats' plans for elections in what became known as the Watergate scandal. The Watergate hearings, a sort of senate trial for the incident, were broadcast on television, and Milk was both angered and dismayed as he watched officials claim that they didn't remember anything when they were asked about their involvement.

Milk felt that the government was in disarray both nationally and locally, and he was just the man to turn things around.

CHAPTER 3

THE MAYOR OF CASTRO STREET

Milk filled out forms to run for San Francisco supervisor just before the deadline. The way in which Milk announced his candidacy would be echoed in the do-it-yourself nature of his campaign: he walked to a plaza in Castro Street, stepped on a crate he had brought with him, and told whomever was out there that he was running for supervisor.

Milk's campaign platform for the 1973 supervisor elections showed just how much he had changed since his days of handing out campaign flyers for Republican presidential candidate Barry Goldwater almost a decade earlier. Milk was very much interested in representing the gay community in San Francisco and being open about his homosexuality, however, he didn't want to run solely on gay rights issues. Instead, he wanted to represent the general interests of San Francisco's left-leaning population.

Milk felt that big business and the tourism industry pulled too much weight in San Francisco.

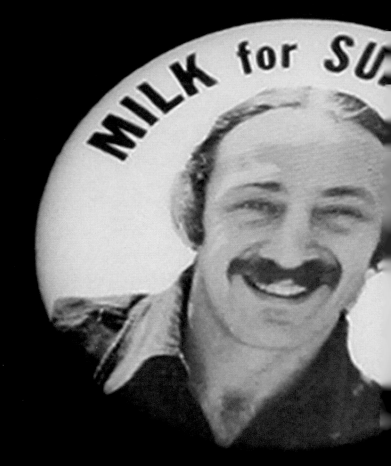

A campaign button from Harvey Milk's first election for supervisor shows Milk, long hair pulled back into a ponytail, before he shed his hippie image.

During this time, the city was working on an airport expansion that Milk felt was out of control, and he wanted to rein it in. Milk wanted to stop the destruction of housing in poor neighborhoods that made way for luxury buildings for the rich. Milk wanted to curb the influence of real estate developers. He was concerned that wealthy, well-connected busi-nesses were taking over the city.

Although Milk's platform was sound, he faced a few major obstacles. The first was getting endorse-ments, in other words, getting orga-nizations and groups to announce support for Milk's candidacy to their members and the public. Another major problem was that Milk had basically no money with which to run a campaign—he had just opened his camera shop, which took the last of the funds he and his boyfriend had. The final impediment was Milk's image. He still looked like the hippie into which he had transformed himself, and his long ponytail made it hard for people to take him seriously as a candidate.

There was, however, one thing for which Harvey Milk had a knack, which this campaign made extremely clear: Milk was very good at delivering speeches. Without the help of a professional speechwriter or professional campaign, and even with a tendency to go off-topic, Milk gave incredibly passionate speeches. He knew how to hold an audience's attention.

Another talent Milk discovered he had was working with the press. He figured out how to get the press interested in his campaign and how to spin everything that happened during the campaign to his advantage. Such talents are how a candidate with almost no money and few endorsements finished tenth out of thirty-two candidates. It was not enough to win it, but it was a very good result for a newcomer with no money.

What's more, the man who had spent so many years going from job to job had, at the age of forty-three, finally found his calling.

MILK'S EVOLUTION

Among the people who marveled at Harvey Milk's transformation was Harvey Milk himself. Despite being gay, Milk led a very conservative life in his early years. He was, in fact, very conservative, politically speaking. During the presidential elections of 1964, Harvey Milk handed out flyers in support of conservative Republican nominee Barry Goldwater.

As a young man, Milk didn't want to make a political issue of being gay. He didn't want to call attention to that part of his life, preferring to keep his personal life private. At this time, he was working on Wall Street and dressing and acting the part of someone working in finance, an industry of suits and discretion.

In the late 1960s, Milk began hanging out with New York's theater crowd, specifically, the experimental theater crowd, whose lifestyles and attire matched the look of the counterculture movement making its way through New York. This was an anticonformist, nonmaterialistic, antiestablishment crowd. In other words, this was a group of people who didn't want to look like and act like everyone else. What's more, they thought that material possessions and money were unimportant.

Milk started growing his hair, only a little at first. Slowly but steadily, Milk began to shed his old political views. He started to get rid of expensive items in his apartment. When he moved to San Francisco the first time, he lived with cast members of *Hair*, a musical about a group of hippies. He attended antiwar rallies. When he worked

(continued on the next page)

(continued from the previous page)

however, he still wore traditional business clothes, but the wall between his two lives was about to come down.

In 1970, when the United States invaded Cambodia, Milk was so angry he attended a protest rally during his lunch break, still in his business suit. In the middle of the crowd, he burned his Bank of America card to symbolize his opposition to American involvement in the Vietnam War.

Milk's hair kept getting longer until his bosses noticed and gave him a choice: he could either cut his hair or quit if he refused. Milk chose neither option and was fired.

When Milk visited New York, he had very long hair and wore beads and fringe; he was a full-fledged hippie. Milk stuck with the hippie look, although not so fully costumed through his first run for office. While he didn't remain a hippie, he would never again be that conservative who wanted to keep gay and lesbian issues a matter for the bedroom only.

NEW CAMPAIGN STRATEGY

Milk had lost his first campaign, but he was by no means ready to give up. He wanted to run in the next election, but he knew he had to make changes to his campaign strategy. For one, he cut off his ponytail and started wearing suits so that people would take him seriously.

But more than his image, the focus of the shift in strategy was relationship building. Milk wanted to make himself better known in the immediate Castro community. He also wanted to work on building relationships that would turn into endorsements by Election Day. An argument between a business and a workers' union would give Milk the opportunity to do just that.

In 1974, beer truck drivers from the Teamsters Local 888, a union, had ended a five-month strike against beer distributors. The distributors didn't like the new contract, but the strike led the parties to an agreement, all except one company—Coors Brewing Company. Coors refused to sign the new contract. In response, the Teamsters organized a boycott. They asked communities and groups in San Francisco to stop buying Coors products. At that point, there was one important group missing from the boycott—the gay and lesbian community.

Allan Baird, a Teamsters member responsible for the boycott, had heard about Milk's influence in the Castro and came to him for help. Milk and Baird made an agreement. Milk would get San Francisco's gay bars to stop selling Coors products and, in exchange, the Teamsters would hire gay drivers. Both sides kept their promises. When the elections came around, the Teamsters supported Milk, and Baird helped Milk get support from other labor unions. This event also demonstrated that the gay and lesbian community was becoming an important, influential group in San Francisco politics.

Milk worked hard to make himself a fixture in Castro life. He'd get up at five in the morning to go

Harvey Milk sits inside Castro Camera during his final and ultimately successful campaign for supervisor. This photo was taken shortly after Milk delivered his "Hope" speech.

out, meet people, and speak to as many groups and organizations as possible. He also created groups and events in the neighborhood, including the Castro Village Business Association and the Castro Street Fair, which became an annual event. Because of his deep involvement in the community, Milk earned a nickname that would stay with him for the rest of his life: the Mayor of Castro Street.

THE POLITICAL WINDS THEY ARE A-CHANGIN'

Milk did not win his second race, the election of 1975, but his hard work did have an effect. He came in seventh, just one place away from a seat on the board of supervisors. For the city as a whole, it was a big night for liberals in San Francisco. A liberal sheriff and two gay-friendly district attorneys were elected into office. That year, there was also a three-way mayoral race, which led to a runoff election between the two candidates with the most votes: a conservative, John Barbagelata, and a liberal, George Moscone. Moscone had been impressed with Milk and his campaign and promised Milk that he would give him a job in his administration if he won the run-off. It was because of the runoff election that Castro Camera became a campaign site for some-one other than Milk—Moscone used it as one of his campaigning sites.

Moscone ended up winning the runoff, just barely. As Moscone had promised, his win meant that Milk got his first taste of a city position. Moscone made Milk one of the members of the board of permit appeals. If someone in the city had a problem or issue surrounding a permit, the board had the final say in resolving the issue.

This appointed position seemed like a good place for Milk to work until the next supervisor election, but Milk couldn't get the idea of winning an elected seat out of his head. When a state assembly seat opened up, Milk was thinking about running for the position, even though he had only been in his new job for five weeks.

SAN FRANCISCO'S SUPERVISORS

The board of supervisors is responsible for proposing and passing laws for San Francisco. The board also votes on which supervisor becomes its president. This role is important not only because the president leads the board of supervisors but also because this person is next in line for mayor if something happens to the current mayor that leaves him or her unable to fulfill his or her duties.

When Milk first ran for office, supervisors were chosen through citywide elections. That is, all residents of San Francisco could vote for any of the supervisors who were running, regardless of where in the city the resident lived. The candidate with the most votes would get the first available seat, the second available seat would go to the next-highest vote-getter, and so on until all available seats were filled.

Many found this system unfair because it meant that candidates with a lot of money and connections had the resources to run big campaigns and make themselves known throughout the city. This situation meant that a disproportionate number of fairly wealthy people represented similar interests and groups. Additionally, there wouldn't be an even spread of representation among the districts. For some districts, not a single supervisor elected to the board came from that district, making it hard for residents there to have their interests represented in city government.

Moscone tried to discourage Milk from doing so. Through a series of deals and promises, the Democrats, including Moscone, already had a

candidate in mind, Art Agnos. Milk disliked the idea
of the political establishment deciding on candidates
through backdoor deals, and he said so in public.
Moscone fired Milk, and the race was on.

It was a hard-fought race, and for a while it looked
as though Milk might win. However, Milk's opponent
was a skillful politician who had the support of the
Democratic establishment. In the end, Milk lost by
thirty-six hundred votes.

RULE CHANGE

By the 1977 elections, Milk had lost three campaigns, but he was not out of the race yet. Milk used
the lessons he had learned from his three losses to
figure out ways to improve his chances next time.
One thing he felt he was sorely missing was the back-
ing of a club. The existing gay clubs in the city did
not support Milk and probably never would, so Milk
decided to create his own club, the Gay Democratic
Club. Its focus was on electing openly gay candidates
to office.

Milk also participated in building a coalition of
very different groups—gays, unions, and activists—
with the common goal of keeping corporate interests
out of politics. It was a marriage of money and voting
power, and the aim was to get a rule change.

The supervisors were chosen citywide, with the
candidates with the most votes getting the available

A joyous Harvey Milk celebrates on the night of his historic election win on November 8, 1977, which made news across the country.

positions. The coalition wanted to structure it so that the race for supervisors would be divided into districts, with each district voting for its own candidates and choosing its own representative. The coalition was able to make this an issue all San Franciscans could vote upon in the next election, and they voted in favor of this proposal. Starting in 1977, candidates for supervisor would run for the position in their own district only.

Each time that Milk had run for supervisor, he had received an overwhelming amount of votes in this district. If all he had needed then was to win his own district, Milk would have been elected.

This election was going to go very differently for Milk than his previous two tries for a supervisor's seat. Even though he was running against other gay politicians in his district, he put all his campaign skills, tricks, and personality into this fight. He even received an endorsement from the *San Francisco Chronicle*; even the newspapers were finally taking him seriously.

On election night, the good news finally came: out of sixteen candidates running in his district, Milk had taken 30 percent of the vote, far more than any other candidate. He finally won. The first openly gay candidate had been elected to office in California. Milk also made national history by becoming the first openly gay man elected to public office in the country.

It was a historic night full of celebration in the Castro. During his victory speech, delivered in a very crowded Castro Camera, Milk spoke of his victory as one not just for gay people but one that could open the door for all minorities.

The next night, Milk paused the celebration for sober reflection and a prophetically dark moment. He made a recording in which he spoke about who he would want to take his place in case something happened to him. Despite the fact that Milk had been elected, there was still a good deal of prejudice and hatred aimed at the gay and lesbian community, and Milk realized that such entrenched attitudes would make him a target.

CHAPTER 4

IN OFFICE

Milk wasn't the only "first" among the board of supervisors to start a new term in January 1978. The board now also had among its members the first Chinese American supervisor, the first African American female supervisor, and the first single mother. Since each supervisor was chosen by his or her district only, the board reflected the diversity of 1970s San Francisco. The board also included a representative from a solidly middle class, blue-collar traditional district: Daniel James White, a former police officer and firefighter. It was a very different board from the ones that had come before it.

Milk proved himself to be a skillful campaigner, but what kind of politician would he be? There were some who had their doubts that he would do a good job in office, that he would be all show and no action. From the early days, however, Milk proved many of his would-be critics wrong.

Milk was no slacker when it came to the duties of his office. He read and researched legislation

Milk laughs after stepping in dog feces, perfectly demonstrating the need for his proposed bill in this classic pooper-scooper incident.

carefully and always came prepared to meetings. His early legislative accomplishments matched his campaign promises. He also worked hard to protect his district from budget cuts. He saved a public library and elementary school slated for closure, and he got daily street cleaning for the neighborhood. His legislation showed his intention to represent the interests of both gay *and* straight people in his neighborhood.

Milk showed an independent streak from the beginning. He liked to vote on his principles, even when unpopular. There were eleven supervisors, and it happened more than once that there would be a 10–1 vote on an issue, with Milk being the only dissenting voice. Milk was not a big fan of the board's president, future U.S. senator Dianne Feinstein. He thought she was not liberal enough and too close to corporations and developers—Milk's real targets of opposition. He did all he could to curb corporations' and developers' influence on government, including trying to push through a higher tax on corporations and introducing a commuter tax on people who lived in the suburbs but worked in the city—that is, people who used city services but didn't pay for them.

MILK MAKES AN ENEMY

In the beginning, Milk struck up an unlikely friendship with conservative supervisor Dan White. Although they had many differences between them,

Dan White, a fellow freshman supervisor, began his tenure on friendly terms with Milk. This relationship would unravel as White nursed a grudge against Milk over a vote on a bill.

White was initially as mistrustful of corporate interests as Milk was. Milk thought White wasn't a bad guy and that his conservative opinions were a result of ignorance. Milk thought White was capable of change and could become a more accepting person. White even voted on Milk's side on many issues Milk supported, including those that centered around gay rights.

The issue that White viewed most important, and one of the main reasons he wanted to run in the first place, was a planned psychiatric treatment center that was going to be built in his district. White was opposed to the institution, believing that it would bring an undesirable element into the community.

The plan was coming up for a vote, and Milk's vote was going to make a difference. With five people planning to vote for and five against, Milk told White that he probably would vote with him. This was, however, before Milk had done his research on the institution. After looking into it, Milk felt the center was needed in San Francisco, especially for troubled young San Franciscans for whom no such place existed in the city. When it came time to vote, Milk voted for the institution, and the measure passed, 6–5.

White was upset. Preventing the institution from going up was the job he had come to do, and he had failed. What's more, White felt Milk had betrayed him. He was so angry that he wouldn't even speak

COURTING THE PRESS

Milk was brilliant when it came to attracting and manipulating the press. He understood that to make the press pay attention to him, he had to, for one, turn himself into a character, someone the press would be interested in naturally. Fortunately for Harvey Milk, this strategy wasn't hard—he was charismatic and comfortable in the spotlight. Also, Milk knew it was important to know people in the media, to make connections with reporters. He did it so well that no other supervisor received as much press attention. Sometimes Milk even came up with ideas for ridiculous policies he knew would never work, just to get media coverage.

Milk could make any subject interesting enough to catch the attention of the press, and he did just that with dog dung. At the time, many people didn't clean up after their pets, and piles of dog feces littered the streets and sidewalks. Milk saw this as a big quality-of-life issue and introduced a bill that would make people clean up after their dogs.

Milk held a press conference to demonstrate to pet owners how to clean up these messes with bags and accidentally (or so it appeared) stepped into a pile of excrement that hadn't been cleaned up—a perfect way to show how widespread this problem was. A photo of the incident made it to the front page of the newspaper. Of course, it likely was no accident, but a well-choreographed publicity stunt.

to Milk for months after the vote. White started to lose interest in City Hall. He spent less and less time there. His behavior at meetings changed, especially when it came to Milk. After the institution vote,

This photo of Harvey Milk and San Francisco mayor George Moscone was taken as the mayor signed the gay rights bill Milk had worked to pass.

whatever legislation Milk was for, White would vote against.

MILK'S FIRST BILL

Milk's legislation would represent the diverse interests of all his constituents, but the first piece of legislation he introduced was a bit more personal. He introduced a gay rights bill. If passed, the bill would make discrimination based on sexual orientation illegal. The bill would prevent discrimination of gays and lesbians in many areas, including employment and housing.

The legislation came at an important time. While the gay and lesbian community had been making slow gains, as demonstrated by Milk's election, there was a growing backlash against gays and lesbians across the country. In the Castro, gays were becoming targets for beatings or worse, as in the case of a young gay couple chased by a gang of men one night in 1977. One of the two men was unable to get away and was brutally murdered. The killer shouted slurs at his victim while stabbing him.

Milk saw a need to protect gay rights not just through empowerment by social pressure but through laws. This type of legislation would help to change the perception of gay and lesbian communities. The newly proposed law was framed in such a way that it wouldn't protect people's right to sexual preference but their civil rights. When the bill came up for a full vote in front of the board of supervisors, there was debate. Some were worried, as they put it, that this bill would okay all sorts of behaviors that some con-sidered deviant. However, when it came time to vote, even those who had voiced concerns voted for it. The final vote, 10–1 for the bill, showed just how influen-tial the gay community had become in politics; the gay vote had become very important for winning elec-tions, and voting against such a bill was politically dangerous. The only "no" vote came from Dan White. Considering this vote came just a week after Milk had voted for the psychiatric center, it was no surprise that White voted against it.

The rainbow flag is a symbol of gay pride. The first version was created in 1978, and the current version was first used in a protest against Milk's assassination.

The only thing left was for Mayor Moscone to sign the law, which he did, with Milk standing beside him. Quoted in a *New York Times* article by Les Ledbetter, Milk said of the law, "This will be the most stringent gay rights law in the country." It was indeed an important bill, coming at a time when gay rights throughout the country were about to be challenged.

VOTE NO ON PROPOSITION 6

In the late 1970s, a singer named Anita Bryant was working with very conservative Christian groups against the gay and lesbian community. They started campaigns to encourage cities to repeal equal rights laws that prohibited discrimination based on sexual orientation. Bryant was an outspoken critic of homosexuality, once suggesting that God allowed a California drought, in part, as punishment for tolerance of liberals and homosexuals. Her movement was garnering a lot of press and gaining momentum. In Dade County,

Anita Bryant, founder of the group Save Our Children, used her fame as a singer to push for laws denying rights to gays and lesbians across the country.

Florida (renamed Miami-Dade County in 1977), a vote to repeal a gay rights bill was passed, and similar repeals began to occur across the country.

Right after the Dade County repeal passed, a California state assemblyman named John Briggs announced his intention to introduce an antigay bill in his state. However, the bill didn't stand a chance in California's assembly, so instead he sponsored an initiative to allow voters to decide whether to ban homosexuals and possibly gay-rights supporters from employment in California public schools. Under California law, certain proposed legislation can be decided by voters on Election Day, rather than by the state legislature. What was called the "Briggs Initiative" became Proposition 6. A "yes" vote would mean that gays and lesbians would be barred from teaching in California public schools.

At first, things didn't look good for the gay and lesbian community and supporters. In early September 1978, a poll showed 61 percent in favor and 31 percent against. Milk and other activists sprang into action. Milk began delivering speeches, speaking out against the measure, and publicly debating Briggs.

During the 1978 Gay Freedom Day Parade, with attendance estimated at more than 375,000, Milk addressed the crowd. He spoke about equality and rights and quoted Dr. Martin Luther King Jr. as well

as the Declaration of Independence. He challenged
President Jimmy Carter to support gay freedom. He
reminded the crowd that America is defined by the
ideal of equality.

An important turning point came when lesbian
and gay activists convinced Republican governor
Ronald Reagan to come out against Proposition 6.
President Carter also publicly stated his opposition.
The unions, with which Milk had worked so hard to
build a coalition, were also against Proposition 6.
The overwhelming momentum of Bryant and her sup-
porters, which seemed so insurmountable in early
September, was now fading. In the end, on Election
Day, November 7, 1978, the electorate voted "no" on
Proposition 6.

CHAPTER 5

TWO MEN DIE, A CITY BURNS

By the time Proposition 6 was defeated, Dan White had lost interest in the board of supervisors. The only law he wanted defeated had passed, souring his opinion of the board and diminishing his enthusiasm for its activities. What's more, he claimed the salary for supervisors, $9,600 a year, or about $35,000 in today's money, made it hard for him to support his family. The combination of these factors led him to resign his position.

A few days after the Briggs Initiative failed, White delivered a resignation letter to Mayor Moscone. White was done with the board of supervisors, or so he thought, until a group of his friends, including policemen and firemen, convinced him to ask for his seat back.

The mayor had the authority to appoint replacements to the board of supervisors and could reappoint White. Initially, Moscone was willing to give White's job back, and he returned White's resignation letter. However, Milk convinced Moscone that that was a mistake, and Moscone found a portion of city law to support his final decision not to reappoint White.

On November 27, 1978, Moscone planned to hold a press conference to announce White's replacement. Although Moscone didn't tell White that he would be replaced, White found out.

White grabbed a gun he owned and headed toward City Hall. There was a metal detector at the front entrance of the building but no detectors at the side entrances. White entered through a side window and headed toward the mayor's office. The mayor let him in for a meeting. White shouted at the mayor, who began to pour White a drink to calm him down. White pulled out his gun and shot the mayor four times, killing him.

White left the office through a side exit to look for Milk, finding him in a hallway. White asked to speak with Milk, and they walked together toward White's former office. As soon as Milk was inside, White pulled out his gun and shot him five times.

Board president Dianne Feinstein, a few doors down, heard the sound of gunfire and went to investigate. She saw White running from his office, and when she got there, she found Milk's body. She felt for a pulse, but, at age forty-nine, Harvey Milk was dead.

THE SAD MARCH TO CITY HALL

A video of that terrible day shows police officers running through City Hall, trying to sort out what had happened. It shows Feinstein standing in front of the press and the public. Her eyes are wide and she looks stunned as she makes the following announcement: "As president of the board of supervisors, it is my duty to make this announcement: both Mayor Moscone and Supervisor Harvey Milk have been shot and killed." There are immediate gasps and cries from the crowd, shouts of "What?" and "No!" When the yelling dies down, she continues: "The suspect is Supervisor Dan White."

"Is he in custody?" someone asks. "He is not at this time," says Feinstein and walks away.

As news of the murders spread, people began to gather at City Hall, placing flowers on the steps and standing silently in shock and disbelief. Flags were lowered to half-mast.

Dianne Feinstein, who became mayor after Milk's and Moscone's assassination, leads a 1979 march in their memory. Feinstein began serving as a U.S. senator representing California in 1992.

In the Castro that day, businesses started to close, many with their doors draped in black cloth. Some store owners displayed photos of Harvey Milk in their store windows. Residents started wearing black arm-bands. The San Francisco Gay Democratic Club, the club Harvey Milk helped to establish, gathered to dis-cuss what they should do. They decided to march to City Hall.

After an impromptu memorial service near City Hall, mourners began to gather in the Castro in the evening, carrying candles. The crowd was massive and growing, eventually numbering in the tens of thousands. It was a slow, quiet march to City Hall, led by a drummer and people carrying flags of the United States, California, and San Francisco. When the mourners reached City Hall, folk singer Joan Baez sang "Amazing Grace," "Swing Low, Sweet Chariot," and other somber songs. When it was over, many mourners left their candles by a statue of Abraham Lincoln.

Later that week, George Moscone's memorial ser-vice was held at City Hall, while Harvey Milk's took place at the opera house, a fitting location, since he had been a lifelong opera fan. Thousands attended each man's memorial service.

Even in death, Harvey Milk still had something to give. His eyes were donated as he had requested. The corneas would be transplanted, giving someone the gift of sight.

The crowd that gathered at City Hall following Milk's and Moscone's assassinations was impressively, poignantly large, spilling into the park and nearby streets.

HIGHLIGHTS FROM MILK'S "HOPE" SPEECH

During his 1977 campaign and subsequent election, Harvey Milk introduced and then perfected a speech that came to represent his reasons for running for office. He delivered a version of this speech time and again in different versions, but the structure and essence of the speech was always the same. After his death, it also became part of his legacy. The speech was born out of politics, but its purpose went beyond. It spoke to the spirit and potential of the gay and lesbian communities around the country and told them not to be afraid.

People working on Milk's campaign came up with a name for the speech, and it stuck: the "Hope" speech. During one occasion when Milk gave this speech, it was recorded, preserving the speech in Milk's own voice.

The speech always began in the same way: "My name is Harvey Milk, and I'm here to recruit you."

Milk would continue with a joke or two and discuss the effects of Anita Bryant's influence on gay rights legislation, but with a positive spin: "For the first time in the history of the world, everybody was talking about it, good or bad. Unless you have a dialogue, unless you open the walls of dialogue, you can never reach to change people's opinion."

Since this was Milk, gay and lesbian rights were not the only thing on his mind, and he would speak about the apartheid in South Africa, or ways in which other minority communities in San Francisco were being affected by proposed policies and legislation.

Milk continued, talking about how important it was to have not only *gay-friendly* people in public office, but gay people themselves. It was important both politically and symbolically to have visible, prominent, and strong gay leadership representing the gay community.

The last part of Milk's speech was where he really transcended politics and spoke to the hopes and fears of gay and lesbian people across the country. He addressed discrimination and physical violence against gay people and the strength of the community as they mourned those they had lost. He talked, finally, about what it ultimately means to have gay representatives in government:

"The only thing they have to look forward to is hope. And you have to give them hope. . . And if you help elect . . . more gay people. . . It means hope to a nation that has given up, because if a gay person makes it, the doors are open to everyone."

THE TWINKIE DEFENSE

White turned himself in to police a few hours after committing the murders. Of the two police officers who recorded his confession, White knew one fairly well. During White's brief taped confession, he claimed that he had never planned on murdering Moscone or White. White claimed that he just happened to take his gun with him and just happened to take an extra box of bullets with him. He claimed he had only wanted to talk with the mayor but that he "got kind of fuzzy" and shot him during their conversation. White claimed that, after killing the mayor and leaving his office, he saw Milk and just wanted to talk with him. But, he said, Milk was "smirking" at him, and this is why White shot him. It was a short confession. Because White was not more rigorously interrogated, many believed the police had gone easy on him because he was one of their own.

White was charged with first-degree murder and a lesser count of manslaughter. If convicted of first-degree murder, White would get the death penalty. His lawyer, Douglas Schmidt, ensured that the jury that was selected had no gay or gay-friendly people serving. He also put a lot of Catholics and middle-class white people on the jury, whom he believed would be sympathetic toward White. Strangely, prosecutor Thomas Norman had twenty-six opportunities to challenge Schmidt's choices but used only six.

Protesters carry signs in front of the Hall of Justice in San Francisco. Inside, Dan White is sentenced to just under eight years in prison.

73

The defense strategy was to argue that White had "diminished capacity," that is, that he wasn't able to think clearly when he committed the murders. To show diminished capacity, the defense used two main arguments. The first was that White was depressed and therefore unable to consider the consequences of what he was doing.

The second point in their defense, which would soon become infamous, was that White wasn't himself because he wasn't getting enough sleep and he was eating junk food. The defense called upon a doctor to testify that White's binging on Twinkies, as White claimed he had been doing, resulted in high doses of sugar, making him violent. This would become known in the press as the "Twinkie defense."

The prosecutor, Thomas Norman, gave a bland opening statement in which he mostly described the chronology of the events that day, without trying to convince the jury that White had planned the murders in advance.

A supervisor who was called to testify told the jury about Milk's history with White and that the killings were politically motivated rather then the result of high sugar levels.

Norman also presented a psychologist, who testified that he couldn't diagnose White with depression and noted that White seemed to feel no remorse for his actions.

THE WHITE NIGHT RIOTS

The trial began on May 1, 1979, and on May 21, 1979, after thirty-six hours of deliberation, the jury reached a verdict. Dan White was found guilty of voluntary manslaughter. It was the only charge on which the jury found him guilty. White was cleared of first-degree murder.

The verdict caused an immediate stir and a great deal of anger. A crowd started to gather in the Castro. Cleve Jones, a friend of Milk's who was now the owner of the white bullhorn Milk liked to use for speeches, grabbed the bullhorn and headed to the streets. Jones galvanized the crowd and led them on a march to City Hall, yelling, "Out of the bars and into the streets!" The people in the bars listened and the crowd grew stronger and began to yell, "Avenge Harvey Milk!"

The crowd headed to City Hall, and by the time they reached it, there were five thousand of them. Waiting at City Hall was a speaker system that had been set up for a planned protest in anticipation of a lenient verdict. The police tried to break up the protest, but the crowd resisted, surprising the police; the gay and lesbian community in the city usually didn't fight back. The community had never gotten this angry so publicly.

Eventually, a rock was thrown through a window at City Hall, and the protest soon turned into a riot.

After the jury reached its decision in Dan White's trial, protesters gathered at City Hall, standing here in front of officers in riot gear.

One group of protesters tried to block the group that wanted to riot. They stood in front of City Hall, preventing the other group from passing. Police arrived, and the group in front of City Hall sat down to show they were peaceful. The police began to beat them, and the crowd retaliated. A police car was set on fire. Eventually every window on the first floor of City Hall had been broken. The crowd threw rocks and bottles at the officers. At first the officers were told not to fight back, but hours later they got the okay. Battles broke out between groups of rioters and police.

Back in the Castro, it was peaceful. Many who
had joined the protest at City Hall had come back
to the neighborhood to avoid the riots, but then
police officers marched in, and without provocation,

The protest turned into a riot, commonly called the White Night riots. Here, participants smash the glass of City Hall's front doors.

smashed the windows of a well-known bar, going on to beat up everyone in the bar. The scene in Castro became as crazed as the one back at City Hall.

When it was all over, about ten hours after it had begun, sixty-one police officers and about one hundred members of the gay and lesbian community had been taken to the hospital. Twelve police cars had been burned. Nineteen rioters had been arrested. The riot had been given a few names, but one stuck: the White Night riots.

As for Dan White, he ended up serving just five years of a seven-year sentence when he was released in 1984. The next year, he committed suicide.

HARVEY MILK LIVES ON

When Harvey Milk was assassinated, the impact his death and life had on the city was evident, from the riots to the peaceful

and large celebration the next day, May 22, on what would have been his forty-ninth birthday. There were other changes as well, ones that didn't include large gatherings of people. The club that he had helped found, the Gay Democratic Club, changed its name almost immediately after Milk's assassination to the Harvey Milk Gay Democratic Club, which it is still called to this day.

In the immediate aftermath of his death, his name, image, and words seemed to be everywhere, especially in the Castro. As time passed, memories faded, especially at the national level. A new

Members of the renamed Harvey Milk Gay Democratic Club march in the 1979 Gay Freedom Day Parade and Celebration in San Francisco, marking the tenth anniversary of the gay rights movement.

Sean Penn is shown here playing Harvey Milk in a scene from the 2008 movie *Milk*. The movie went on to win Academy Awards for Best Actor and Best Original Screenplay.

generation arrived, and Harvey Milk was no longer a household name.

In 2008, however, a movie called *Milk* was released in theaters. Starring Sean Penn, it told the story of Milk's life, beginning just before his move to San Francisco. It introduced Harvey Milk to a new audience, and his name was once again on everyone's lips.

That didn't mean, however, that his name had disappeared before the movie came out. It was around, but in more subdued ways.

One organization that carries on Milk's legacy is the Harvey Milk Foundation, created in 2009 to spread Milk's story around the world. The foundation was started by Milk's nephew, Stuart Milk,

and Anne Kronenberg. Stuart is the son of Milk's only brother. Like his uncle, Stuart is an openly gay activist. Anne Kronenberg was the campaign manager during Milk's final and successful campaign for supervisor. Kronenberg had not only been Milk's political colleague but also a friend.

The foundation was established with the advice and memories of Milk's old friends and gets his message of hope to different communities in many ways. Stuart Milk and Kronenberg travel around the world delivering speeches on Milk's legacy to large government groups and at small community gatherings. An exhibit about Harvey Milk's life was created in partnership with the California Museum in Sacramento. The foundation also wrote a play that is performed in schools and campuses across the country.

HOW TO BE AN LGBT ALLY

For a person who is not LGBT (lesbian, gay, bisexual, and transgender), becoming an LGBT ally is an important way to make sure that all individuals are afforded the respect, safety, and support they deserve.

There are many different ways to be an ally. You can show your support for and acceptance of LGBT people you know, or you can be an activist and speak out for LGBT rights. For someone struggling with gender identity or struggling to make the decision to come out, having a friend who accepts him or her no matter what can be a very big deal.

One important step to becoming an ally comes through education and understanding. It is important to learn about LGBT issues and the kinds of thoughts and fears running through the minds of people making the difficult decision to come out of the closet. Understanding and sympathy can go a long way. When it comes to learning about LGBT issues, try to diversify your resources: it's good to do online research, but talking to your LGBT friends about their experiences can be equally eye-opening.

Institutional support can also be important. Many schools have gay-straight alliance organizations, comprised of LGBT youth and allies, providing a safe space for students. If your school doesn't have a group like this and you're interested in starting one, organizations such as Gay-Straight Alliance provide resources, assistance, and advice for creating a gay-straight alliance organization.

Speaking up and explaining to people that their anti-LGBT jokes or negative comments are hurtful can be very powerful. It is often difficult and nerve-wracking to confront someone behaving this way, but it gets easier with experience and gives other people courage to speak up as well.

Finally, once you've gained experience as an ally, you can help others who want to become allies. Getting as many people as possible involved in ending prejudice, stereotyping, hate, and violence that many in the LGBT community face sends a powerful message that these hurtful acts are completely unacceptable in a just society.

A NAME THAT ENDURES

Harvey Milk's name and image appear in ways large and small. In San Francisco, an elementary school in the Castro now bears his name—the Harvey Milk Civil Rights Academy, which celebrates diversity and teaches tolerance in addition to regular subjects. In New York City, the Harvey Milk School provides a refuge for LGBT high school kids. Back in California, a few of the places now named after Harvey Milk include the Harvey Milk Recreational Arts Center, the Harvey Milk Institute, and the Eureka Valley/Harvey Milk Memorial Branch Library.

One of the most fitting tributes to opera-lover Harvey Milk was *Harvey*

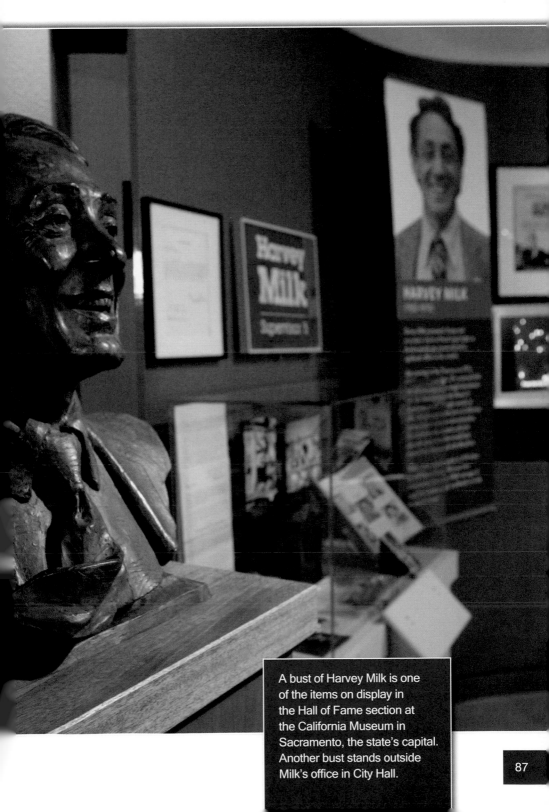

A bust of Harvey Milk is one of the items on display in the Hall of Fame section at the California Museum in Sacramento, the state's capital. Another bust stands outside Milk's office in City Hall.

Milk, the opera. A joint production by the New York City Opera and the San Francisco Opera, the show premiered in 1995 with a run in both San Francisco and New York City. The opera told Milk's story from his early years to his death.

Back in the Castro, one of the plazas where people gathered in the aftermath of his assassination is now called Harvey Milk Plaza. In City Hall, on what would have been Milk's seventy-eighth birthday, Milk's former friends, politicians, and the public gathered for an unveiling: a bust of a grinning Harvey Milk, now permanently installed at City Hall, a first for a supervisor.

In 2009, the state of California ensured Harvey Milk's name would be remembered in the state for a very long time when Governor Arnold Schwarzenegger signed into law a bill that created Harvey Milk Day. It is celebrated every May 22, Milk's birthday. While not a state holiday, it is one of four special days California has on its books. In addition to serving as a remembrance to Harvey Milk, during this day schoolteachers are encouraged to educate students about Harvey Milk so that his name is recognized and the significance of his life and work understood.

The celebration however, is not limited to California. On Harvey Milk Day, communities and groups across the country host their own events, from a diversity breakfast in Orlando, Florida, to a day of service in Pittsburgh, Pennsylvania.

The Presidential Medal of Freedom is the highest honor that can be bestowed upon a civilian. Each year, the president identifies individuals who have made extraordinary contributions to society, and recipients are awarded the medal in a special ceremony. In 2009, Harvey Milk was chosen to receive the honor. Since it was awarded posthumously, or after his death, his nephew Stuart Milk received the honor on his behalf.

Harvey Milk's name would surface in the White House again a few years later, when President Obama honored ten individuals as the Harvey Milk Champions of Change. The honorees were LGBT politicians who had made a difference in their communities.

In ways large and small, on the local and national level, Harvey Milk's name and memory live on.

MILK'S LEGACY

It is impossible to know what would have happened to Harvey Milk if he hadn't been assassinated. He certainly had his eye on bigger, more prominent roles in government. Perhaps if his life hadn't been cut short so abruptly, Milk would have added a few more firsts to his résumé: the first openly gay president of the board of supervisors, the first openly gay mayor. We will never know.

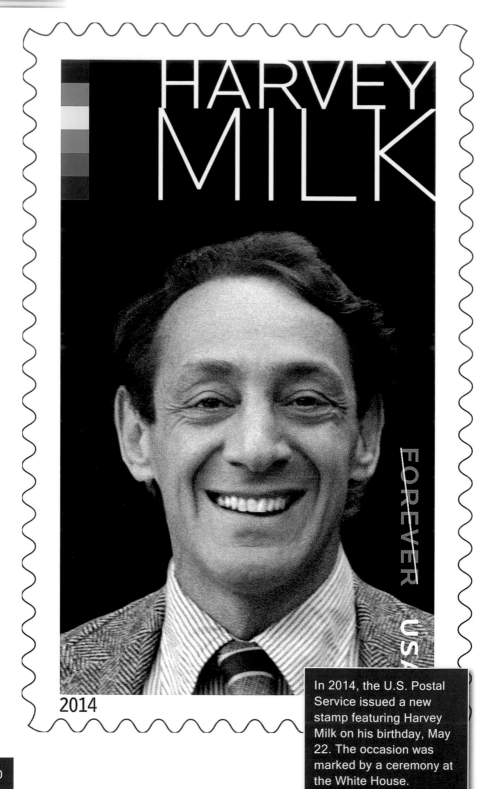

HARVEY MILK

FOREVER USA

2014

In 2014, the U.S. Postal Service issued a new stamp featuring Harvey Milk on his birthday, May 22. The occasion was marked by a ceremony at the White House.

What we do know, however, is that in his short life and during his brief ten months in office, he made an impact that improved the lives of the people in his community, gay and straight.

His "Hope" speech encouraged people across the country who were struggling in so many ways: with being open about their identities; with living in a society where homosexuality was often viewed as a sin or a mental disease; with families who were intolerant and unaccepting; with laws that sought to exclude them from certain jobs merely for being gay or even for being suspected of being gay. One of the most famous lines from that speech was, "You gotta give 'em hope," and Harvey Milk did.

We can't know what Milk might have accomplished had his life not been cut short, but in life and death he would be a symbol, and Milk knew this. This was the point of his "Hope" speech: he knew someone had to embody that hope, to show it was possible for one member of the LGBT community to accomplish his dream of being elected as an openly gay, political representative, so that all members of the LGBT community would feel empowered to do the same.

This is why Harvey Milk continues to be such an important figure—why his name, his birthday, and his legacy continue to be celebrated.

TIMELINE

1930 Harvey Bernard Milk is born on May 22 in Woodmere, New York.

1947 Milk graduates from high school.

1951 Milk graduates from college in June.

Milk joins the navy shortly after graduation.

1956 Milk meets Joe Campbell.

1969 Milk moves to San Francisco for the first time in September.

1970 Milk is fired from his job for having long hair.

1971 Milk moves back to New York, where he works as an associate producer on a Broadway play.

1972 Milk moves back to San Francisco.

Milk settles on Castro Street in October.

1973 Milk opens Castro Camera on March 3.

Milk runs for the board of supervisors for the first time. He loses the race for supervisor on Election Day in November.

1974 Milk works with the Teamsters to support a boycott of Coors Brewing Company.

1975 Milk runs for supervisor for the second time. He loses the election on Election Day.

1976 Milk is appointed to the Board of Permit Appeals by George Moscone and has his swearing in ceremony on January 30.

Milk decides to run for state assemblyman in March and is fired from his position on the Board of Permit Appeals. He loses the state assemblyman election.

1977 Milk runs for supervisor for the third time. He wins the race for supervisor and is the first openly gay man elected to public office in November.

Shortly after winning, Milk records a message explaining whom he would like to take his place if he is assassinated.

1978 Milk is sworn into office on January 9.

Mayor Moscone, with Harvey Milk by his side, signs the antidiscrimination bill—the first bill Milk introduced—into law on April 11.

Milk speaks at the Gay Freedom Day Parade in San Francisco and talks about the damage the Briggs Initiative could do.

The Briggs Initiative (called Proposition 6) is defeated on Election Day, thanks in part to Milk's opposition.

Dan White resigns from the board on November 10.

Dan White assassinates Mayor Moscone and Harvey Milk on November 27.

ACTUARIAL Of or relating to statistical calculation, especially of life expectancy.

ASSASSINATE To murder a prominent person for political reasons.

AVENGE To get even with or retaliate on behalf of someone else.

COALITION An alliance of different politicians or political parties in order to achieve a common goal.

CONSERVATIVE Someone who believes in a limited role of government and has traditional values.

CONSTITUENT Member of a district who is represented by an elected official.

COUNTERCULTURE A culture that differs from the norm and often rejects traditional ways of thinking and behaving.

DIMINISHED CAPACITY A defense in criminal law in which the defendant argues he or she should be found guilty of a lesser crime than the one committed due to mental impairment or disease.

DISSENTING Describing an opinion that is the opposite of another.

EMPOWERMENT Giving power, authority, or permission to.

ENDORSEMENT Formal support of a particular candidate in an election.

ENLIST To sign up for the armed forces.

EXTORTION The use of force or threats to get something, such as money, from a person.

GALVANIZE To get people excited or encourage them to take action.

HIPPIE A usually young person who rejects established society (e.g., by dressing unconventionally) and believes in nonviolence.

IMPROMPTU Made or done without preparing ahead of time.

INCUBATOR A space that allows ideas to develop and grow.

INSURMOUNTABLE Incapable of being overcome, as an obstacle.

INTRAMURAL Occurring within the limits of an organization or institution, as in sports competitions among students at the same school.

LEGITIMATE Legal, proper, or done according to the rules.

LGBT Coined in the 1990s, LGBT is an acronym standing for the lesbian, gay, bisexual, and transgender community.

LIBERAL Someone who believes government should be active in supporting social and political change.

NEUROTIC Tending to worry in a way that is not healthy or reasonable.

OUT OF THE CLOSET An expression used to describe someone who is openly gay.

OUTSIZED Something bigger than normal or larger than life.

PERCEPTION The way that something is viewed or understood.

PERMISSIVE Giving people a lot of freedom to do what they want to do.

PLATFORM In a political campaign, a candidate's beliefs, opinions, and ideas about an issue or topic.

POLITICAL ESTABLISHMENT A group or party that holds power and influence.

PRESUMPTUOUS Being bold or forward in a way that doesn't seem justified.

PROVOCATION An action or occurrence that causes someone to become angry or act out.

SUNY An acronym standing for State University of New York. Established in 1948, SUNY is a state-supported system of higher education with over fifty campuses throughout New York.

TRANSCEND To rise above or go beyond typical boundaries.

FOR MORE INFORMATION

American Civil Liberties Union (ACLU)
125 Broad Street, 18th Floor
New York, NY 10004
(212) 549-2500
Website: http://www.aclu.org
The ACLU works to preserve the constitutional rights
of all Americans and fights for the rights of
communities—such as the LGBT community—
that historically have been denied rights given to
other communities.

The Center: The Lesbian, Gay, Bisexual &
Transgender Community Center
208 West 13th Street
New York, NY 10011
(212) 620-7310
Website: https://gaycenter.org/home
The Center offers health and cultural programming
for the LGBT community and maintains a multi-
media archive of the community dating from
the 1920s.

GLAAD
104 West 29th Street, #4
New York, NY 10001
(212) 629-3322
Website: http://www.glaad.org

GLAAD monitors and uses the media to ensure the LGBT community is portrayed positively. GLAAD provides reports and information about members of the LGBT community in the media, plus ways to participate and celebrate in LGBT events.

GLBT Historical Society
657 Mission Street, Suite 300
San Francisco, CA 94105
(415) 777-5455
Website: http://www.glbthistory.org
The GLBT Historical Society provides research and information about the history of the GLBT community in San Francisco and beyond.

Harvey Milk Foundation
P.O. Box 5666
Fort Lauderdale, FL 33310
Website: http://www.milkfoundation.org
The Harvey Milk Foundation, founded by his nephew, Stuart Milk, and his campaign manager, Anne Kronenberg, aims to spread social and political equality for individuals of all genders, sexual orientation, races, ethnicities, and ages.

Human Rights Watch (HRW)
350 Fifth Avenue, 34th Floor
New York, NY 10118

(212) 290-4700

Website: http://www.hrw.org

Human Rights Watch supports and defends
oppressed groups and communities around the
world. The LGBT section of HRW's website provides reports and information about HRW's work
with LGBT communities.

The Pride Library

The Pride Library, D. B. Weldon Library

First Floor, Room 107

The University of Western Ontario

London, ON N6A 3K7

Canada

(519) 661-2111

Website: http://www.uwo.ca/pridelib

The Pride Library collects and makes publicly available works written by or for the LGBT community.

San Francisco Museum and Historical Society

The Old Mint

88 Fifth Street

San Francisco, CA 94103

(415) 537-1105

Website: http://www.sfhistory.org

The San Francisco Museum and Historical Society
researches and documents the history of San
Francisco.

Supporting Our Youth (SOY)
333 Sherbourne Street, 2nd Floor
Toronto, ON M5A 2S5
Canada
(416) 324-5077
Website: http://www.soytoronto.org
SOY provides help, support, mentoring, programming,
   and housing and employment opportunities for
   GLBT youth in the Toronto area.

WEBSITES

Because of the changing nature of Internet links,
Rosen Publishing has developed an online list of
websites related to the subject of this book. This
site is updated regularly. Please use this link to
access the list:

http://www.rosenlinks.com/LGBT/Milk

Ashbolt, Anthony. *A Cultural History of the Radical Sixties in the San Francisco Bay Area.* London, England: Pickering & Chatto Ltd, 2013.

Bérubé, Allan. *My Desire for History: Essays in Gay, Community & Labor History.* Chapel Hill, NC: The University of North Carolina Press, 2011.

Black, Dustin Lance. *Milk: A Pictorial History of Harvey Milk.* New York, NY: Haymarket, 2009.

Bronski, Michael. *A Queer History of the United States.* Boston, MA: Beacon Press, 2011.

Bronski, Michael, Ann Pellegrini, and Michael Amico. *"You Can Tell Just by Looking" And 20 Other Myths About LGBT Life and People.* Beacon, MA: Beacon Press, 2013.

Daley, James, ed. *Great Speeches on Gay Rights.* Mineola, NY: Dover Publications, Inc., 2010.

Eaklor, Vicki L. *Queer America: A People's GLBT History of the United States.* New York, NY: New Press, 2011.

Elinson, Elaine, and Stan Yogi. *Wherever There's a Fight: How Runaway Slaves, Suffragists, Immigrants, Strikers, and Poets Shaped Civil Liberties in California.* Berkeley, CA: Heyday Books, 2009.

Foley, Michael Stewart. *Front Porch Politics: The Forgotten Heyday of American Activism in the 1970s and 1980s.* New York, NY: Hill and Wang, 2013.

Gay, Kathlyn, ed. *American Dissidents: An Encyclopedia of Troublemakers, Subversives, and Prisoners of Conscience.* Santa Barbara, CA: ABC-CLIO, 2012.

Handhardt, Christina. *Safe Space: Gay Neighborhood History and the Politics of Violence* (Perverse Modernities). Durham, NC: Duke University Press, 2013.

Keat, Nawuth. *Alive in the Killing Fields: Surviving the Khmer Rouge Genocide.* Washington, DC: National Geographic Society, 2009.

Lee, Chang-Rae. *The Surrendered.* New York, NY: Riverhead Books, 2010.

Lynch, Janet Nichols. *My Beautiful Hippie.* New York, NY: Holiday House, 2013.

Maupin, Armistead. *Tales of the City.* New York, NY: HarperCollins, 1971.

Milk, Harvey. Jason Edward Black, Charles E. Morris III, Frank M. Robinson. *An Archive of Hope: Harvey Milk's Speeches and Writings.* Berkeley, CA: University of California Press, 2013.

Moon, Sarah, ed. *The Letter Q: Queer Writers' Letters to Their Younger Selves.* New York, NY: Scholastic, 2012.

Ridinger, Robert E., ed. *Historic Speeches and Rhetoric for Gay and Lesbian Rights (1892–2000).* New York, NY: Routledge, 2012.

Roque-Ramirez, Horacio N. *Queer Latino San Francisco: An Oral History, 1960s–1990s.* Hampshire, England: Palgrave Macmillan, 2014.

Schall, Rebecca. *Historic Photos of San Francisco in the 50s, 60s, and 70s.* Nashville, TN: Turner Publishing Company, 2010.

Stone, Amy L. *Gay Rights at the Ballot Box.* Minneapolis, MN: University of Minnesota Press, 2012.

Weiss, Mike. *Double Play: The Hidden Passions Behind the Double Assassination of George Moscone and Harvey Milk.* 2nd ed. San Francisco, CA: Vince Emery Productions, 2010.

Wolf, Sherry. *Sexuality and Socialism: History, Politics, and Theory of LGBT Liberation.* Chicago, IL: Haymarket Books, 2009.

Brandon, Katherine. "Presidential Medal of Freedom Recipients." Whitehouse.gov, July 30, 2009. Retrieved August 12, 2009 (http://www.whitehouse.gov/blog/2009/07/30/presidential-medal-freedom-recipients).

Buchanan, Wyatt. "S.F. Prepares to Unveil Bust of Harvey Milk." SFGate, May 22, 2008. Retrieved February 12, 2014 (http:// www.sfgate.com/bayarea/article/S-F-prepares-to-unveil-bust-of-Harvey-Milk-3283379.php).

California State Legislature. *SB-572 An Act to Amend Section 37222 of the Education Code, and to Add Section 6721 to the Government Code, Relating to Harvey Milk Day.* California: October 11, 2009.

Carlsson, Chris, ed. *Ten Years That Shook the City: San Francisco 1968–78.* San Francisco, CA: City Lights Books, 2011.

Chan, Sewell. "Film Evokes Memories for Milk's Relatives." *New York Times*, February 20, 2009. Retrieved January 24, 2014 (http://cityroom.blogs.nytimes.com/2009/02/20/film-evokes-memories-for-harvey-milks relatives/?_php=true&_type=blogs&_php=true&_type=blogs&scp%20=2&sq=mendales&st=cse&_r=1).

De Anda, Juan. "Throwback Thursday: Harvey Milk Assassination: November 27, 1978." *San Francisco Examiner*, November 28, 2013.

Retrieved February 2, 2014 (http://blogs
.sfweekly.com/exhibitionist/2013/11/throwback
_thursday _harvey_milk.php).

Emery, Vince. "The Unknown Adventures of Harvey
Milk in Dallas." Dallasvoice.com, May 17,
2012. Retrieved January 25, 2014 (http://www
.dallasvoice.com/unkown-adventures-harvey
-milk-dallas-10113520.html).

Fitzgerald, Frances. "The Castro I." *New Yorker*,
July 21, 1986.

Geluardi, John. "Dan White's Motive More About
Betrayal Than Homophobia." SFWeekly, January
30, 2008. Retrieved February 2, 2014 (http://
www.sfweekly.com/2008-01-30/news/white
-in-milk).

Harder-Markel, Donald P. *Out and Running: Gay
and Lesbian Candidates, Elections, and Policy
Representation.* Washington, DC: Georgetown
University Press, 2010.

Ledbetter, Les. "Bill on Homosexual Rights
Advances in San Francisco." *New York Times*,
March 22, 1978.

Linder, Douglas O. "The Trial of Dan White: An
Account (The 1979 Trial for the Murders of
Harvey Milk and George Moscone)." Famous
Trials, 2011. Retrieved February 6, 2014
(http://law2.umkc.edu/faculty/projects/ftrials/
milk/milkhome.html).

Lindsey, Robert. "Dan White, Killer of San Francisco Mayor, Suicide." *New York Times*, October 22, 1985. Retrieved February 6, 2014 (http://www.nytimes.com/1985/10/22/us/dan-white-killer-of-san-francisco-mayor-a-suicide.html).

Milk, Harvey, and Vince Emery, ed. *The Harvey Milk Interviews: In His Own Words.* San Francisco, CA: Vince Emery Productions, 2012.

PFLAG. "Guide to Being a Straight Ally." Parents, Family and Friends of Lesbians and Gays, 2007. Retrieved February 15, 2014 (http://community.pflag.org/document.doc?id=139).

Pogash, Carol. "The Myth of the 'Twinkie Defense.'" SFGate, November 23, 2003. Retrieved June 13 (http://www.sfgate.com/health/article/Myth-of-the-Twinkie-defense-The-verdict-in-2511152.php).

Rimmerman, Craig A. *From Identity to Politics: The Lesbian and Gay Movements in the United States.* Philadelphia, PA: Temple University Press, 2002.

San Francisco Public Library. "Letters from Harvey Milk to Joe Campbell." Retrieved January 24, 2014 (http://sfpl.org/index.php?pg=2000186701).

Shilts, Randy. *And the Band Played On: Politics, People, and the AIDS Epidemic.* New York, NY: St. Martin's Press, 1987.

Shilts, Randy. *The Life and Times of Harvey Milk: The Mayor of Castro Street.* London, England: Atlantic Books, 1982.

State University of New York at Albany. "Harvey Milk, '51: From Intramural Athlete to Civil Rights Icon." March 2, 2009. Retrieved January 24, 2014 (http://www.albany.edu/news/campus_news_5680.php).

Tran, Mark. "Arnold Schwarzenegger Signs Law Establishing Harvey Milk Day." *Guardian*, October 13, 2009. Retrieved February 6, 2014 (http://www.theguardian.com/world/2009/oct/13/schwarzenneger-law-harvey-milk-day).

INDEX

ABOUT THE AUTHOR

Corinne Grinapol is a writer living in Brooklyn, New York, who has previously written books for Rosen Publishing.

PHOTO CREDITS

Cover © Ronald Grant Archive/Alamy; p. 7 Robert Clay/ Ambient Images/Newscom; pp. 10–11 SuperStock/ Getty Images; pp. 12–13 spirit of america/Shutterstock .com; p. 16 Harvey Milk Archives-Scott Smith Collection, Gay & Lesbian Center, San Francisco Public Library; pp. 20–21 Everett Collection/SuperStock; pp. 24–25 Justin Sullivan/Getty Images; p. 30 Mickey Pfleger/Time & Life Pictures/Getty Images; pp. 32–33 Gene Forte/Hulton Archive/Getty Images; pp. 36–37 Danny Moloshok/Reuters/Landov; pp. 42–43, 51, 53, 56–57, 60–61, 66–67, 69, 72–73, 76–77, 78–79, 80–81, 86–87 © AP Images; p. 47 © Robert Clay/ Alamy; p. 59 Dan Henson/Shutterstok.com; pp. 82–83 © AF Archive/Alamy; p. 90 U.S. Postal Service/AP Images; cover and interior graphic elements © iStockphoto.com/traffic_analyzer (colored stripes), © iStockphoto.com/rusm (pebbled texture).

Designer: Nicole Russo; Executive Editor: Hope Lourie Killcoyne; Photo Researcher: Amy Feinberg